The RACE

Marked Out for Us

A STUDY GUIDE BY DOT BOWEN

THE RACE
Marked Out for Us

A Note From Your Coach

If you believe you are not a runner, then you're in good company. I thought the exact same thing! I have told everyone who will listen that I hate running and I hate exercise.

The author of Hebrews writes, "Therefore, since we are surrounded by such a great cloud of witnesses, let us throw off everything that hinders and the sin that so easily entangles. And let us run with perseverance the race marked out for us." Hebrews 12:1 (New International Version)

Whether we feel like it or not, God says that we are runners. And while I don't claim to have all the answers, God has graciously taught me many truths about how to run this race called life. I'm so glad that you have decided to come along with me in this training program! Are you ready to learn a few of the things God has taught me about how to run this race, or rather, how to live the life He has called us to live?

We may not run along similar paths, but every child of God is called by Him to run their own personal race. Of course, we can find encouragement from other runners who have been running longer and learned to become the best runners they can be. I pray you will find in this training a group of women who will encourage you to pursue the life God has designed for you with purpose and passion.

To begin, the first thing we must do is embrace our race. Often we will struggle with the temptation to compare our race with that of others. Remember, your race is personal and designed especially for you. God will give you the grace to run your own race with Him. So, let's ask God to show us how to run the race He has called us to run. Since it is God who has called us to run, it will be God who will provide all we need to run with endurance. There's no greater "running manual" than God's Word. God created and set us in our race with a plan and purpose. We must be wise and seek Him for further instructions on how to run that race well.

You may feel you have no energy to run. Or maybe you've never understood why your journey has been paved with such pain and heartbreak. I am sure if I knew the path you have been asked to run, I would feel the same way. I pray this training will give you a fresh wind of endurance, and a new beginning as you seek His truth and fall more in love with the Jesus of the scriptures. I believe the more you discover the truth of who Jesus is, the more you'll discover the woman He created you to be!

So grab your Bible, your pen, and remember to pray before starting any running program. God looks more at your heart than He does your technique. And one last suggestion: Don't forget to receive and drink water from Jesus. He will offer you His living water throughout your journey and it's up to you to drink!

Let's get ready to embrace life and run!

Dot

How to Use the Study Guide

The purpose of this training manual is to enhance your desire to know the true God, to love Him unconditionally, to follow Him faithfully, and to embrace who you are as His child. I believe this is only possible when we embrace the life God has designed for us, accept who God says He is, and believe we are who He says we are as His children.

Running a race can be used as a metaphor for living the life God has designed specifically for each of us. Throughout the New Testament, Paul compares a follower of Jesus to an athlete, and the life of a believer to a race.

There is no greater example of what it means to be a follower of Jesus than that of a runner in a race that God has set.

Each "rule" in this study guide corresponds to a chapter in my book, *The Race Marked Out For Us*, and has scripture, commentary, and life application questions to help you become a more faithful runner in the race you have been called to run. Please take time each day to pray, reflect, and ask God to show you how to apply His Biblical truths to your life. It is my prayer that by the time you complete this 10-part program, you will be more in love with Jesus, embrace your race with joy, and discover the real you!

Finally, you will see the following "running terms" used in each chapter as learning tools for this training. This will help you digest essential truths as nourishment to your heart and soul. In my experience, it doesn't matter how much I train if I don't receive and digest the proper nutrients along the way. My life will not work until I apply the nourishment of His truth within the circumstances of my life.

Please get acquainted with each running term that we will be using throughout the training program.

Running Terms to Remember

Your Race-Your Life-Your Story —
Before every race, a runner examines the path marked out for her. In each section, we will take time to examine the past and present journey of your life. In other words, we will use the details of your story to determine your current running program.

Mile Markers —
We will define and examine major life-changing events throughout your journey, the choices made at a fork in the road, or major circumstances that changed your life forever.

Mental Preparation —
Often the determining factor between winning and losing a race is our mental status. Healthy thinking is vital to healthy living. We will examine the thoughts we allow to enter our minds and determine if we're embracing truth or lies so we can train accordingly.

Heart Monitor —
As a runner in this race called life, we often determine our success by the outcome of the race. But as children of God, our success is determined by the condition of our hearts. Throughout the training program, we will stop often and check the condition of our hearts.

Nutrition & Hydration —
No matter how much you train, your body and your life will only work with the proper nutrients from the word of God. Water is essential in helping you to run with the endurance to avoid becoming weak and weary. So we will learn what it means to drink from the springs of living water offered by Jesus.

Community —
You were meant to enjoy community. Every runner enjoys having a little encouragement with a few cheerleaders along the way. We will build our support group with runners who can offer us Godly advice & wisdom from experience.

Rest & Recovery —
After every race, it is vital to one's health to stop running and seek rest. It is important as a child of God to find your rest in the goodness of God. Our recovery time will be determined by the amount of rest we allow our hearts to receive from Him. Rest and recovery occur when we stop running from God and start running to Him

CHAPTER ONE

You Had Me at Hello

YOU HAVE BEEN CREATED AND
CALLED BY GOD TO RUN THE
RACE HE HAS SET FOR YOU.

Therefore, since we have so
great a cloud of witnesses
surrounding us, let us also
lay aside every encumbrance
and the sin which so easily
entangles us, and let us run
with endurance the race
that is set before us.

Hebrews 12:1 (NASB)

As we begin this study, let's start with the most foundational principle:

We have been created and called by God to run the race He has set for us. Each of us has a starting point, a lane in which we run and a course that has been carved specifically for us.

The day I decided to sign up for a half-marathon, I had no clue what I was doing. I didn't understand all the things a runner needed to know in order to run well. The same is true of my decision to follow Jesus. When I said yes to Him, I had no clue what it really meant to follow Him. The writer of Hebrews encourages every follower of Jesus to throw off anything that hinders and the sin that so easily entangles. This means getting rid of anything that keeps us from running the race God has set for us. But what does that mean? How do we throw off hindrances in a practical way? How do we run this race?

The first rule to living the life God has offered is to know that we were created by Him and called to have relationship with Him. We are not on this earth to live for ourselves, but for Him. We have been wonderfully made in His image to bring glory to Him. How can we embrace this truth so that it helps us on a daily basis? We can find the answer in Genesis 2 and Psalm 139.

Take some time to meditate on Genesis 2 and Psalm 139. Take note of how these two passages help us embrace the truth.

We're about to embark on a journey of study, and preparing for this journey will require spiritual discipline. It may also require us to identify ourselves in a new way.

Let's identify ourselves as runners.

For the moment all discipline seems painful rather than pleasant, but later it yields the peaceful fruit of righteousness to those who have been trained by it.

Hebrews 12:11 (English Standard Version)

Your Race Your Life Your Story

—

I remember going to church for the first time with my aunt at her small Baptist church and hearing the preacher talk about hell. I knew that I did not want to go to hell, so I decided to ask Jesus into my life. Jesus dying for my sins and giving me a "get out of hell card" was all I knew the day I said yes to His call. That's what my faith was about at first.

Tell your faith story and where you are in your faith today. When did your race begin, and how are you different now than from the time you first decided to give your life to Jesus?

When did you first understand you had been created and called by God for a purpose? What would you say your purpose is in life?

Mile Markers

It has been many years since I ran Disney's half-marathon and yet, it seems like yesterday. I didn't know what I was signing up for, but I had lots of expectations. As a new follower of Jesus, I had a similar list of great expectations. I expected a life free of pain, tears, and heartbreak while I waited for heaven. I was wrong again! Both of these events were life-altering decisions I will never forget.

It's not unusual for life to be fine one minute and then change on a dime, for better or for worse. What are some of your life-altering events that may have come on suddenly and changed you forever?

When those life-altering events happened, how did they impact the way you viewed God? What kinds of questions did they cause you to ask?

Are there any other important mile-markers you had to face that have changed your life forever? Just to get you thinking, I have listed a few examples.

Your parents' divorce
Your divorce
Moving to a new city
The death of a loved one
Change in financial status
Physical health issues
Emotional disorders
Aging parents
Addiction

Other _____

If this list awakens a wound, try to push through to see how God has used your experience for your good and His glory. As hard as these things are to live through, can you see God's hand in it? If so, how has God used these difficult situations to lead you to His purpose in your life? In other words, if these things had not happened, what might you have never known?

_____

_____

_____

*If you cannot see God's purpose in your circumstances yet, that's ok. Even if you're still in the middle of a difficult or painful situation, you can trust that His word is true and lasting, and He **will** work things together for your good and for His glory.*

Romans 8:28 (English Standard Version)

Mental Preparation

—

I thought being a follower of Jesus was an escape from hell. That was my biggest concern and the most interesting thing about the relationship with him at first. Much like my decision to run the half- marathon, I was more interested in the escape than the actual race. The idea of having a vacation with my grandkids and enjoying the spa was a beautiful picture, but it was not accurate. We often build the same kinds of ideas around our life with Christ before we come to see that, just like my dreams of Disney, our ideas are a far cry from reality.

When I accepted Jesus' call to follow Him, I thought that meant life was going to be easy because I was now following a powerful God. What expectations did you have when you first started following Jesus? How have they changed, or how has reality proven different as you've run your race?

It took a long time for me to under- stand the difference between my experience in coming to know Jesus as Savior and the experience of His forgiveness through His act of love. One was rooted in fear, and the other was motivated by love. Right now, which would you say you are more motivated by in your relationship with Christ: fear or love? Why?

What are your tendencies when handling circumstances out of your control?

Heart
Monitor

—

We talked about what happened in the garden in Genesis 2, when Adam and Eve thought God was withholding something from them. They wanted to take matters into their own hands, which is when things got out of control.

What are your tendencies when handling
circumstances out of your control?

Has there ever been a time when you felt God
was withholding something from you? If so,
describe that time and how you felt toward God.

Take a moment to answer this question in total
honesty: What are the deepest desires of your heart?

Has God said "no" to any of these desires?
Do you trust God with them? Why or why not?

Nutrition & Hydration

———

As we talked about in the video, Adam and Eve were the very first runners! They ran away from God after eating of the fruit, and we've all been running ever since. We run toward what we think will fulfill us, satisfy us and give us joy. The desire to be loved and accepted, and the longing to live life with purpose, are godly desires. What is not godly is seeking to fulfill these desires with things other than God.

**To whom or what do you run to meet your needs
when you feel unloved, unforgiven, and unworthy?**

Community

—

Who are the people you are running with at the moment? Do they encourage you to be faithful to the call God has placed on your life?

Who do you listen to for advice in your personal life?
What about encouragement in your spiritual life?

Do you think the way you live your personal life impacts
your spiritual life, and visa versa? Why or why not?

Rest &
Recovery

—

"Then God said, 'Let us make man in our image, after our likeness. And let them have dominion over the fish of the sea and over the birds of the heavens and over the livestock and over all the earth and over every creeping thing that creeps on the earth.' So God created man in his own image, in the image of God he created him; male and female he created them."

Genesis 1:26-27 (ESV)

Reflect on this question:

Why would God want to create a man and a woman?

It's not as if God needed man for any purpose. God is complete in who He is. God did not need man to bring Him value or importance. God is sufficient in who He is, but He wanted to have a relationship with us.

Take a few minutes to read the story of creation in Genesis 1 and 2. Do you notice God enjoying all He created and calling it good?

After that, God rested. I don't think God was tired. I think God rested to enjoy all He had created.

And He created us to follow the same pattern: resting in Him and enjoying His presence.

We can rest in what we do know: God created us to have a relationship with Him, and His desire has never changed. God enjoys us and He wants us to enjoy Him. Do you?

You may have many questions still unanswered, but one thing you can know is that you are created by God and called to a purpose that isn't found in *what you do for God, but that you belong to God!*

Rest and recover in these truths:

Read Romans 8:22-30

I really love Romans 8:28-30. Notice the words "called" and "purpose."

Rest in the truth of His great love for you!

How hard is it for you to be still and rest in the greatness of God? Do you find enjoyment in being still, or do you find it difficult?

God placed man and woman in the garden, and their purpose was to take care of the garden, name the animals and walk with God. From the beginning and before the fall, mankind was given a purpose. Adam and Eve knew their purpose. They knew what God wanted and did not want. We know they eventually disobeyed God, but even in disobedience they knew their purpose. Do you feel like you know yours?

How could resting in this truth change the way you view yourself, your relationship with God, and your work in the world?

CHAPTER TWO

The Training Program

YOU MUST UNDERSTAND AND
APPLY BIBLICAL TRUTH IN
ORDER TO RUN FAITHFULLY.

For physical training is of some value, but godliness has value for all things, holding promise for both the present life and the life to come.

1 Timothy 4:8 (NIV)

If there is one thing I learned in my experience with the half-marathon, it is the importance of training. When I registered for the race, I had every intention of training, although I can't say I truly understood the importance of it. My understanding was shaky, but my intentions were good. I wanted to run (or at least walk) before the day of the race, but those intentions never came to fruition. I know now that if you hate to run it's easy to allow everything you would rather do come before training.

When I first became a follower of Jesus, I didn't own a Bible. I was running on whatever was offered to me in church. I thought this was enough because I didn't understand the importance of scripture. Again, my understanding was shaky but my intentions were good. In time, I realized I needed to seek and hear from God myself, so I bought a Bible and started to read His words. Specifically, I started reading the book of John in the gospels.

When I said yes to Jesus, I went to church because I thought going would make Him happy with me. I searched the Bible to find something to make me feel better about myself. For most of those early years I acted like Jesus was following me. I would lead the charge and when things took a turn for the worse, I expected Him to jump in and rescue me. I approached scripture much the same way, looking for verses to validate what I wanted.

For years, I didn't know the truth in 2 Timothy 3:16:

All Scripture is breathed out by God and profitable for teaching, for reproof, for correction, and for training in righteousness.

2 Timothy 3:16 (ESV)

Did you grow up learning Bible stories? When did you begin
to study Scripture for yourself, or is it something you do?

Underline the word "training" in both 2 Timothy 3:16
and Hebrews 12:11. How do you think Scripture trains
us to live within our current circumstances?

Your Race
Your Life
Your Story

—

How did you view the Bible before you became a follower of Jesus?

How did your view of the Bible change when you became a Christian?

How has realizing the importance of God's truth written
in Scripture changed your life or impacted your faith?

Mile
Markers

—

What were the lessons you learned about yourself,
about your purpose, and about God after walking
through a very difficult time in your life?

How did God use that season or those
circumstances to train you as His follower?

How did Scripture help you in that season?

Mental Preparation

—

In the space provided, write Hebrews 12:11. Then read the verse out loud. Meditate on every word. What do you think the writer of Hebrews was saying concerning training?

Heart Monitor

—

How do you respond when your life doesn't turn out the way you planned? When you are disappointed by friends, family, or even God?

Is it easy for you to push anger to the side, or do you struggle with anger issues? What about resentment or bitterness?

Have you ever considered these circumstances may be some of the things God is using to train you in righteousness?

Nutrition & Hydration

—

I'm going to list a few ways God will provide the proper nutrients needed to help you understand how to train to your potential. Oh, how I wish I knew these when I first started running the race as God's child! It's never too late to learn how to train. Remember, God uses different avenues to train each of His children.

Bible Study	2 Tim 3:16
Church	Acts 16:13; Acts 11:26; 1 Cor 5:4; Matt 16:18
Ministry	1 Peter 4:10; 1 Tim 1:12; Eph 6:7
Circumstances	1 Thess 5:18; Eph 6:16; Phil 4:12-13
Discipline	Heb 12:5-11; Rev 3:19; 1 Cor 9:27
Testing Faith	2 Cor 13:5; Heb 11:7; 1 Peter 1:7
Suffering	Acts 5:41; Acts 9:16; Rom 8:17-18; Phil 1:29; 1 Thess. 3:4; 2 Tim. 1:12; 1 Peter 2:20-21; 1 Peter 3:14-17; 1 Peter 4:16-19
Community	1 Cor. 12: 12-14, 26; Eph 4:12

Community

Where did you learn how to study the Bible? Who has taught you the most about how to live as a follower of Jesus?

Would you say that you are surrounded with people who value God's Word? If so, how does this impact your life on a daily basis?

Rest & Recovery

—

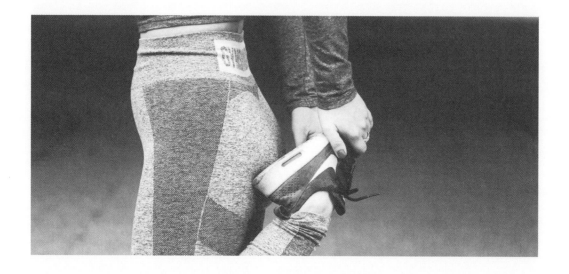

I continue to remind myself if I truly believe the truth of who Jesus is, I will run to Him instead of running from Him. Do you agree? If so, how can you rest in Him today?

**Rest in the truth of Matthew 11:28-30. Read this
passage and write it in the space provided.**

**How do we "come to Jesus?" Prayer is a gift we have been given to enter into the
presence of God. Jesus said, "Learn from me." How does He describe who He is?**

CHAPTER THREE

When You Don't Know What to Do, Go Shopping

WE SHOULD REMOVE FROM OUR
LIVES ANYTHING THAT WOULD GET
IN THE WAY AND THE SIN THAT SO
EASILY HOLDS US BACK.

We are destroying
speculations and every
lofty thing raised up
against the knowledge of
God, and we are taking
every thought captive to
the obedience of Christ.

2 Corinthians 10:5 (NASB)

I was shocked when I realized I would be leaving for Orlando within a few days. I was to run the half-marathon at Disney, but I had spent no time in preparation. I almost had a panic attack! My choice in the face of such panic? Go shopping. I believe this is what people refer to as "retail therapy." Clearly, I needed to be more concerned with running than I was with clothing, but it was the thing I could control in the moment. I hadn't trained, but I could look like I had. In the end, it really wasn't about the clothes; it was about fitting in. Can you relate?

When we don't know what to do, we sometimes do whatever is within our control to make it seem like we know. This behavior only highlights our tendency to hide instead of stand in the freedom of Christ and see our lack of resources as a perfect opportunity to find the abundance of His. Let's dig into what it looks like to embrace this third principle and remove anything that gets in the way or holds us back.

Your Race
Your Life
Your Story

—

What do you do when things get tough? Do you find yourself hiding behind certain activities to keep from dealing with difficult situations? Are you a "stuffer" when life is challenging, or do you process by talking it all out? Let's try to identify our patterns when life gets stressful and anxiety starts to creep in.

Examine your past and present journey in life. Have you ever been in a situation where you felt you did not belong? Describe it.

How did you respond in that situation? How did you feel?

Mile Markers

—

After ignoring countless emails reminding me to train for my upcoming race, I decided to shop for new clothes. And while I was shopping I ignored the sales associate who wisely suggested not buying new clothes for a race.

**Describe the most recent time you can remember
when you did not listen to wisdom.**

What were the consequences you reaped as a result?

What were your feelings toward God in the midst of those consequences?

Mental Preparation

—

I have to admit, shopping has been a way of escape for me. However, "retail therapy" can lead to the problem of overspending, not to mention the guilt that comes when your priorities feel out of balance.

How do you cope with stress or the
feeling of being overwhelmed?

What is your preferred method of escape? What
are some of the repercussions of that escape?

What makes it difficult for you to set your
mind on what is important to God?

What's one thing you can do to start fighting
the lies the world tells you are important?

Heart
Monitor

—

Think about a moment where you were simply looking the part or faking it until you made it. This may even be your current reality. When have you dressed like a runner, but under the surface, haven't trained for your race?

What deeper issue in your heart or your life were you trying to cover up?

I felt abandoned by God after my dad died and I hated to admit it at the time. If you have ever felt that God abandoned you, can you share that experience?

Nutrition & Hydration

—

It doesn't matter how much you train your body; your life will only work with the proper nutrients from the word of God.

Listed below are a few verses for you to soak into your heart and mind. Memorize one of these this week and try to imagine how your life would change if you applied these truths to your life.

Read Genesis 3 to dig deeper into Adam and Eve's "great cover up."

Galatians 3:26-27

Ephesians 4:22

Ephesians 4:25

Ephesians 6:11-17

Colossians 3:12

Colossians 3:14

Community

─

Because of my lack of training, I felt I had to at least look the part in order to run the race at Disney. This experience helped me realize that I carried this same pattern into my relationship with other Christians. How about you? Do you know someone who tries very hard to be the perfect Christian? Often when we're in this mode, we get busy with a lot of doing. However, the Christian life is not in the doing, it's in the being.

The salesperson tried to tell me a real runner never buys anything new to wear before a big race but I would not listen. Along my path as a follower of Christ, there have been a few sincere Christians who have shared truth with me, and, at the time, I did not listen. I thought I would be the exception to the rule. I have never escaped the consequences of walking in ignorance. Have you?

How would you describe the difference between "doing" and "being?"

The church is full of people who are hiding behind busyness to mask their lack of understanding of the heart of God and His will for their lives. Do you struggle with this?

I mentioned dressing like a runner to cover up my lack of training. As a follower of Jesus, I covered up my insecurities by saying "yes" to every volunteer position at church. Have you ever done something like this?

We know that God and His word are our ultimate source of wisdom and comfort, but God also uses others ahead of us on the path to speak truth into our lives. Who are some experienced runners in your life? What qualifies them to speak into your life?

Rest & Recovery

—

Rest in the truth that you are important to God. He wants you to be you, and He encourages you to not compare yourself with another. Will you rest in Him?

Look at your calendar and see what you may need to eliminate in order to have more time in prayer and Bible study. Are you willing to give God everything you have tried to hide from Him and others? True freedom is being honest and authentic before God. He is the ONLY one who will accept you unconditionally. He knows all about you! It is Jesus who will be real with us if we will only take the time to stop hiding.

Take a moment to confess to God where you are pretending or hiding.
Ask God to remove the facade you have put in place that keeps you from
enjoying the fullness of His love, despite your circumstances or trials.

Take a moment and be real with God. Make a list of emotions or feelings that may be causing you to feel abandoned by God. Then, make a list of some attributes of God you know are true. How do the lists compare?

CHAPTER FOUR

It's Never Too Late to Start

WE MUST BEGIN USING OUR PAST
AND PRESENT CIRCUMSTANCES AS AN
OPPORTUNITY TO TELL THE STORY OF GOD.

Brothers and sisters, I do not consider myself yet to have taken hold of it. But one thing I do: Forgetting what is behind and straining toward what.

Philippians 3:13-14 (NIV)

I really could not comprehend how all the stretching at the starting line could help anyone run a race, although it was good entertainment that made the time go by faster. Standing with my coffee probably wasn't the best decision either. Looking back, I can see that there were elite runners, good runners, and wanna-be good runners, and each of us had one thing in common: We all had to start from the same starting line.

Today we are exploring the truth that it's never too late to start! When life becomes too hard to keep moving forward, our first temptation is to quit. Instead of quitting, I would love to encourage you to take the first step and move forward with a new awareness. You have a God-story that needs to be told, and you are the only one who can tell it.

Together, let's take the first step and begin by embracing our race. I'm talking about the life God has asked YOU to live! It may not be the life you thought you would live, but to someone who needs to hear your story, it could bring the hope they need.

Your Race
Your Life
Your Story

—

I would love to talk with the apostle Paul for so many reasons. When I read his sweet encouragement to the church at Philippi in Philippians 3:13-14, I want to ask him, "Are you speaking from experience?" How did Paul not allow his involvement in the deaths of so many Christians to keep him from moving forward? Can you imagine the shame and guilt Paul could have felt when he remembered the death of Stephen and the deaths of so many other Christians he was personally responsible for? But there's no evidence in any of his writing that he allowed his past to keep him from moving forward in his call to proclaim Jesus as the Messiah. If Paul could forget his past and move forward, don't you think God also wants us to forget the past and move forward into what He has ahead for us?

Has shame and guilt from your past produced a fear that
someone might judge you for what happened then?

Do you believe that God can use your story to encourage
someone close to you or even someone you barely know?

Think about your own redemptive story. Share a portion of your
story and think about how God can use it to encourage others.

Has there been a longing in your heart and soul to move forward and
invest in someone's life? What has kept you from taking that first step?

Let me say this: I am a firm believer that no one should tell every sinful detail of her past. God is Who we need to confess our sins to, and we can embrace His forgiveness. However, we need to share how God has rescued, redeemed, forgiven, and changed our lives forever with the people who the Holy Spirit leads us to.

You don't have to share every sin you have ever committed. You only need to tell what God has done, not what you have done. This is a starting point for everyone to learn how God can use all our stories. Trust me! I understand it's hard to know when or what to say to the person who might need to hear your story. The way I have handled this is by asking God to speak through me and allow me to be sensitive to His leading. He will help me know how much detail I need to share, and I can lean heavily into expressing God's forgiveness and redemptive power in my life as I do.

Here is a good guiding question:

Will what I'm about to share leave the person thinking more about the sinful details or the forgiving power of God?

You never want anyone to remember the sinful details. Instead, you want them to be encouraged with the forgiveness of God.

When you hear someone tell you God wants to use you
in the lives of others, do you believe that to be true?

Do you struggle with feeling unworthy?

Paul wrote almost the entire New Testament. How would
the Christian faith look different today if Paul allowed
his past mistakes to keep him from proclaiming that
Jesus the Messiah died for our sins and we are forgiven?

Let me ask you again: If God leads you to, are you willing
to share with someone what God has done in your life?

What message is God writing on your heart to share?
Can you write it in a few sentences?

Mile Markers

My daughter Christy made me aware that if I didn't make it to a certain mile marker at a certain time in the race, someone would come sweep me up and deposit me at the finish line. I would not be able to finish the race if that happened. My response to her was one of sheer stubborn will. I would NOT allow anyone to end my race prematurely! When I made that decision, it became the power that pushed me to run in a way that I was simply not prepared to run. This was a huge mile marker for me in the race.

Reflect back over a few mile markers (life-changing events) in your life. Our response to life's changing events can either display God's greatest power in our lives, or it can leave us discouraged and in despair.

When I was standing at the starting line, it was easy for me to say what I would do to keep running, but things changed once I was running. It's easy to say how we will respond until we are living right in the middle of the difficulty. Can you relate?

If you're comfortable sharing, write down a few life-altering mile markers (good and bad!) that have occurred in your own life.

I don't think anyone escapes this life without experiencing some sort of life-altering circumstance. The question is not if you will, but how you will. How have you responded in these events? How are you responding at this moment?

Mental Preparation

—

Finally, brothers and sisters, whatever is true, whatever is noble, whatever is right, whatever is pure, whatever is lovely, whatever is admirable—if anything is excellent or praiseworthy—think about such things.

Philippians 4:8 (NIV)

I remember studying this verse as a young runner. I knew I needed to obey God and choose to think on His truth, but I didn't know how. For some reason I found it very difficult to keep my mind from negative thinking. Do you struggle with keeping your mind free of negative thoughts?

What thoughts do you struggle with that are in opposition to this command in Philippians?

How do you see your thoughts guiding your perspective?

I shared with you how I would hear other people's success stories and how their lives seemed to be perfect. Watching how others were living for Jesus made me feel like I could never measure up and be like them. This did not motivate me to try to live better; it discouraged me from trying at all!

How about you? Have you struggled with any of the thoughts listed below?

If only I had her husband....

If only I had their financial status...

If only I had their family...

If only I had her looks...

If only _____

Remember, we will never be perfect in controlling our thoughts but we can get better at it. Ask God to protect your mind and help you choose what you allow to enter into it.

What is your "if only" that is keeping you from God's best?

How would your thoughts look different if you embraced
Paul's command to think on what is true?

Heart Monitor

—

I have found I have to constantly check the condition of my heart if I am to live the life God has asked me to live. If we don't take time to monitor our hearts, we risk allowing bitterness to destroy everything we love. This has happened to me. Have you ever been so bitter toward someone, or even God, that it made it difficult to love other people (or God)?

I asked my son one time why he uses a heart monitor while running different races. He said he has to pace himself because he never knows when he will have to run uphill. He never knows when he will face an uphill struggle. There is so much truth in this for our spiritual lives, too!

In life we never know what lies ahead. If we don't keep a current check on the condition of our hearts, we may unexpectedly face a mountain that we are not only too weak to run, but could cause us to lose the will to go on.

No matter what the condition of your heart while you are running your race, it's important to always be aware of where you have allowed your heart to go.

Take a moment and reflect on where you've allowed your heart to wander. Then, let the Holy Spirit gently guide you to the springs of living water that Jesus is offering you.

What is the condition of your heart at this moment?

Do you need God to replace a heart of stone with a heart that trusts Him?

Nutrition & Hydration

Shame and guilt will take a toll on your heart if you allow them to remain. Read and reflect on these scriptures and ask yourself, "Do I believe this?" If you believe what God is saying, then embrace the truth and drink from Him! If you are struggling to believe them, confess this to God and ask Him to help you know these truths in your life.

As you look these verses up, write down what you believe God is saying to you. Put His words in your heart.

Matthew 22:37-40

John 14:1

John 14:27

Mark 12:29-30

Mark 8:17-18

Community

Waiting at the starting line, drinking my coffee, surrounded by thousands of runners eager for the race to start, I actually felt like a runner for a brief moment. Unfortunately, it was only a feeling. In reality, I was not a half-marathon runner!

I was surrounded by all different levels of runners, but I did not become a runner until I started to run. We all have to start somewhere. I believe we must assess where we are in our race and embrace that place, wherever it is, allowing God to teach us how to keep running.

I also believe God will use other people who have learned what it means to run with God. This is exactly why I wrote the book. I wanted to share the lessons and mistakes I learned as an untrained runner and also in my life race as a child of God. Hopefully, you will learn from my mistakes and run in such a way that you win the prize, enjoying the life God has asked you to live.

If you have no one who can encourage you to run your race, stop now and ask our Father to send someone to help you learn the truth of how to live/run in the race of life.

Maybe there are others around you who need to be spurred on. Is God calling you to be a cheerleader for someone else? How can your God-story encourage them in their race?

Do you feel alone, even as people are running their own races all around you?

Read Hebrews 12:1-2 again and think about the "cloud of witnesses." These were some of the first cheerleaders! How do their stories encourage us today?

Who are your greatest cheerleaders?

Rest & Recovery

—

I have given you several verses throughout this study guide. Take a moment from running and meditate on the Word of God. Rest in His love for you. No one will ever love you as fully and unconditionally as God does. Today, read:

John 3:16

John 10:10-17

CHAPTER FIVE

Are You Thirsty?

CONTENTMENT, PEACE AND
SATISFACTION ARE ONLY FOUND
WHEN WE ALLOW THE SPIRIT OF GOD
TO FILL OUR THIRSTY SOULS.

Finally, brothers and sisters,
whatever is true, whatever
is noble, whatever is right,
whatever is pure, whatever is
lovely, whatever is admirable—
if anything is excellent or
praiseworthy—think about
such things.

Philippians 4:8 (NIV)

I know what it means to be physically thirsty, and I know what it means to be spiritually thirsty. Both have the potential to rob you of your life.

What I saw within minutes of starting my half-marathon was outright shocking to me. People were going out into the open field and emptying their bladders! I couldn't believe this was a viable choice for them. A few minutes later it made more sense. I came upon a row of port-a-potties where the lines were as long as those for the most popular roller coasters in the park. It didn't take me very long to see that there were no good options for me during the race. Stopping wasn't an option, even to use the restroom. At my age, using an open field or standing in a long line for a bathroom break didn't seem like wise choices for me. So I did what I thought was wise at the time: I chose not to drink water during the race. This, of course, was NOT a wise choice, and I got so thirsty! I have never been so physically thirsty in my life!

The definition of thirsty is... "a strong or eager desire to do or have something you long for and desire very much."

What are you thirsty for? Do you have a strong and eager desire that has not been met? Never underestimate the power of an unmet desire or expectation. Eventually, those desires can take total control of your mind, heart and soul. I know! I was deceived into thinking that things other than Jesus could satisfy the longing of my heart. Once again, I was wrong!

Every decision and choice I made at the beginning and during my race seemed right at the time. Yet again, I was wrong. I've told you my story. Now, would you like to talk about yours?

Are you comfortable talking about the deep desires of your heart? The best person to talk this over with is Jesus. It's not like He doesn't already know, but He has offered you a place at His feet to share with Him what you are really seeking. Don't let this opportunity pass by.

Your Race
Your Life
Your Story

—

As you look back over your life, how have you tried to quench your own thirst by drinking from man-made wells filled with polluted water? (Polluted water is anything the world offers to satisfy your human desires.)

What have you longed for in your life but never received?
What have you thirsted for?

Do you find it hard to wait on God to fulfill the desires of your heart?

Mile
Markers

—

What event in your life would you consider a life-changing
moment where you took matters into your own hands?

How did that turn out? What were you looking for
that made you choose to try to handle it on your own?

At the root of your thirst, is there a current or past
circumstance that has left you feeling alone or depleted?

Mental Preparation

—

Often when we are looking to people for acceptance or to circumstances to give us validation, we are responding to a wrong pattern of thinking.

Can you write down a few things you believed to be truth,
only to find out later they were actually lies that you embraced?

Has it been a difficult process changing negative thinking
into positive thinking based on truth from God's Word?

Heart
Monitor

—

To be thirsty means to long for something or someone to satisfy the desires of your heart.

**Do you believe that Jesus is the only
One who can satisfy your thirst?**

What does that mean in your life right now?

**What would surrendering to God to satisfy the
desires of your heart look like in a tangible way?**

**What are you thirsting for in this season
that requires you to trust Him?**

Nutrition & Hydration

—

Nothing was going to satisfy my thirst the day of the race except for water, pure and simple. I decided to take a bite of a protein bar, but it may as well have been dirt in my mouth. It only served to magnify how thirsty I was.

Jesus says:

"Whoever drinks the water that I will give him will never be thirsty again."

John 4:14 (ESV)

Take a moment to reflect on this Scripture. Are you attempting to quench your thirst with other things? Make a list of things you've hoped would quench your thirst but only enhanced your craving.

Why is it sometimes easier to go to these
things instead of the water of life?

Community

Do you find it easier to get your needs
met by others than to wait on God?

How are your relationships with other people impacted
when you try to have all your needs met by them?

Who in your life fills you up and points you back
to the Living Water when you are depleted?

Rest & Recovery

—

After a long day of running to and fro, it's time to rest in the truth of God's Word. Here are a few truths for you to read, believe and apply. Take a sip from the water Jesus is offering and drink of the living water.

And the LORD will guide you continually and satisfy your desire in scorched places and make your bones strong; and you shall be like a watered garden, like a spring of water, whose waters do not fail.

Isaiah 58:11 (ESV)

Jesus said to her, "Everyone who drinks of this water will be thirsty again, but whoever drinks of the water that I will give him will never be thirsty again. The water that I will give him will become in him a spring of water welling up to eternal life."

John 4:13-14 (ESV)

The Spirit and the Bride say, "Come." And let the one who hears say, "Come." And let the one who is thirsty come; let the one who desires take the water of life without price...

Revelation 22:17 (ESV)

As I approached every water station along the path during the half-marathon, I was offered water, but I refused to drink.

The same is true in the race God has set for you and me. God may allow others to offer us His truth in different ways, but we can always find water in the pages of Scripture. The water of life (Jesus) will not satisfy our souls until we drink. What will you choose?

CHAPTER SIX

My Own Cheering Squad

IF WE ARE TO RUN OUR OWN RACE,
WE MUST BE CAREFUL OF THE
VOICES WE LISTEN TO.

Therefore encourage one another and build each other up, just as in fact you are doing.

1 Thessalonians 5:11 (NIV)

I got so exhausted trying to run a race that I had no business running in the first place. I tried to draw strength from eating a protein power bar, and when this did not help, the cheers of the crowd gave me a short-term boost of energy. The determining factor in my race was lack of water, not the cheers of the spectators. The crowd was not running my race; I was. How could they possibly know what I needed to finish strong? As a matter of fact, they should have told me to stop, turn around, and drink water!

Unfortunately, applause and approval from others have very limited power to replace the power of God in a person's life. I have discovered over the years that if you look long enough, you will find someone who will encourage you to go in a direction God never intended. Since God has mapped out the right path for you, He is the only One who knows the direction and path you should be running. I have never known a "crowd" to be a good source of wisdom. The only crowd I would even consider listening to is listed in Hebrews 11. The heroes and great runners of the past are known for their faith, not their experience.

Your Race
Your Life
Your Story

—

Do you have a "running story" where you were going down the wrong path, and instead of being surrounded by people with wisdom and discernment who encouraged you to change direction, you were surrounded by people who encouraged you to do the wrong thing?

As you look back on your life, do you think you would have a different story if you
had listened to Godly advice or surrounded yourself with faithful followers of Jesus?

Read and write 1 Corinthians 10:11-13.

What truth can we take from the words Paul wrote to
the "runners" at Corinth concerning temptation?

If God has promised to make a way of escape and the power to walk away from temptation,
why do you think so many of us still give into the temptations we face every day?

What happens when you give into temptation or listen to someone
who you later discover doesn't have your best interests at heart?

Mental Preparation

Throughout my life I have had to contend with truth vs. lies. So many times I've held onto ideas as truth when in reality, they have been destructive lies. In my half-marathon, I wrongly thought I could run 13.1 miles without training or drinking water. As a follower of Jesus, I also had a wrong view of what it meant to be His follower. It is important for us to take a good look at the beliefs we hold and determine if they are based in God's truth, or if they are lies that have crept in.

Take a moment and list a few of the lies you have believed
about the heart of God and His desires for you.

Mile Markers

The Apostle Paul, a great runner in God's race, encourages us to not keep looking back on our past regrets but to move forward to the life God has for us (Philippians 3:13-14). I truly believe that what we set our eyes on, we go to. If we focus on our past regrets, chances are we will repeat them. On the other hand, it's wise to learn from our mistakes so we don't make them over and over again.

Are you okay with "glancing" back on a few of your past races? If you can, list some of the obstacles that were in your path. It could be people you let in your life, feelings you ignored, or places you knew not to go.

Look back on a few defining moments in your life. Try to identify moments where you paid attention to the nudge telling you to be careful where you were going. Can you see where God provided a way out of your circumstance?

What about a time when you didn't pay attention to the warning signs. How did it turn out?

I will never forget the day I read Romans 6:21. I'm not going to spoil it for you and tell you what it says. Instead, I'll ask you to read this passage and answer the question it asks for yourself.

Heart Monitor

—

I believe it's extremely dangerous to begin your day without checking the condition of your heart. How can we examine the condition of our hearts? When we realize we are weary, tired, and discouraged, or heading down the path to despair, we likely have a heart issue. I try to check my heart before I get in the "danger zone" by taking a few minutes to be still before God in prayer. Through prayer and reading your Bible, you can ask God to show you the true desires of your heart.

It is in those moments that I ask the Holy Spirit to reveal to me if there's something I long for that is not from Him. If something comes to mind I say, "God I'm giving you my heart," and I ask Him to give me His desire and help me to want only what He has for me. Often it's hard for me to understand why God says no to something I have asked of Him. I'm learning that when God gets hold of my heart, the "why" behind His refusal to give me what I asked for isn't as important any more.

Can you express the desires of your heart to God?

I have heard women say they are afraid to express their desires to God
for fear of being disappointed by Him. Have you ever felt this way?

If you are struggling with trusting God and are afraid to give Him every part of your heart,
take a few moments and sip on the truths listed in the Nutrition & Hydration section. These
truths can renew, replenish, and give you everything you need to mend a broken heart.

Nutrition & Hydration

—

For the LORD God is a sun and shield;
The LORD bestows favor and honor.
No good thing does he withhold
from those who walk uprightly.

Psalm 84:11 (ESV)

Think about this: If God was willing to send His Son to die for you so you could have a personal and loving relationship with Him, why would He refuse to give you anything other than His best?

Sip on this throughout the day:

> **"God is a good Father who protects, leads, and directs His children."**

We all know a "good Father" who truly loves his children will eventually have to say no to anything He understands has the potential to hurt the child.

If you then, who are evil, know how to give good gifts to your children, how much more will your Father who is in heaven give good things to those who ask him!

Matthew 7:11 (ESV)

Community

If you have been hurt by someone you believed to be a dear friend, remember Jesus understands your pain. It's never wise to follow the crowd. How many times can a mom tell her child this? How many times can God tell us?

Here's a challenge:

Jot down something that's happening right now in your life, an area in which you need wisdom, comfort or peace.

Now write down who you could and/or would most likely call for input on the subject at hand. Take that list of names and set them aside for now.

We all know God can provide us with wise counsel through the mouths of others, But today, take a moment to silence those other voices, as comforting as they may be. Go before your Heavenly Father and invite Him in as your FIRST line of defense. Ask the Lord to direct you in this place. It's okay to feel the silence in the room around you, as it can often open your heart to really hear from the Lord. He desires to speak to His children and provide the wisdom and the "cheering" you may need today.

I have friendships that have spanned over 30 years, friends who have proven to love and accept me unconditionally. Yes, we may have a few people in our lives who will pray for us, encourage us to obey God, and will give us godly wisdom, but these friends will not be found in a crowd. These friends are only found when they are going in the same direction we are — running to Jesus.

When I heard the crowd cheering on the sidelines, I truly thought they were there to encourage me to keep running. It's ridiculous now to think complete strangers were waiting for me to come around the corner just to cheer me on. I'm going to go ahead and admit it: I saw these cheering strangers as my friends. It's okay, you can laugh!

There is a reason God tells us not to put confidence in man. Read the story of Jesus and you will discover that He, too, was disappointed by his friends.

At first, the crowd was singing His praises. In Mark's gospel he writes, *"Many people spread their cloaks on the road, while others spread branches they had cut in the fields. Those who went ahead and those who followed shouted, 'Hosanna! Blessed is he who comes in the name of the Lord!'" Mark 11:6-9 (NIV)*

Yet in the days that followed, the crowd was yelling "Crucify him!" No, these weren't Jesus' close friends. So what did his close friends do?

Peter, who declared he would never disown Him? We know how that turned out! A rooster crowing marked three times that Peter denied Him. As Jesus was being flogged and carrying His cross, His disciples fled. Judas sold Him out for a small amount of money. When Jesus came out of the grave, not one of His friends were there waiting, even though He told them often that He would rise again.

Have you ever thought you could trust someone only to find out later they were not trustworthy? Write about it in die space below.

Rest & Recovery

—

Look over everything we talked about today and rest in the truth given throughout this chapter. Allow your heart to receive what God is saying. Truth will set you free only when you obey the truth given to you!

CHAPTER SEVEN

The Finish Line

EVERY CHOICE WE MAKE WILL IMPACT
NOT ONLY OUR LIVES BUT ALSO THE
LIVES OF THE PEOPLE WE LOVE.

Do not be deceived, God is not mocked; for whatever a man sows, this he will also reap.

Galatians 6:7 (NASB)

I was tired, weak, and weary. I tried to find strength on my own terms. My body needed water, and I refused to drink what I was given. As I continued to run by my own rules, I was losing way more than the race. The consequences of all the choices I made before and during the race met me at the finish line, affecting the outcome of the race and bringing fear and heartbreak to my family.

To remind you of the sub-title on this chapter:

Every choice we make will impact not only our lives but also the lives of the people we love.

The choices I made were never intended to hurt anyone. And even though they were made from a pure heart, I couldn't stop the consequences of my choices. As followers of Jesus, our choices about how we live our lives can sometimes come from a pure and loving heart but still be made in ignorance.

The truth is that consequences have nothing to do with forgiveness. We are loved and forgiven by God, but in the race called life, our choices will always carry consequences.

My choices were driven by my lack of understanding. My lack of understanding led me to believe I could do something I had no business doing. It's not that I didn't have faith; it's that I had faith in the wrong thing! The same is true in my Christian life. I fail every time I put my faith in anything or anyone other than Jesus.

Your Race
Your Life
Your Story

—

No one can avoid consequences. We may not experience the pain of our poor decisions until later, but the truth of the matter is we will never be able to outrun consequences. The good news is this applies to the good choices we make as well. In time, we will reap what we sow, usually later and often more than we sowed in the first place.

As you consider "reaping and sowing," think about the different areas in your life and the choices you are now making concerning your health, your career, your friends, your family, and your relationship with God.

Do you understand the difference between reaping the consequences
of your choices, and God's forgiveness for the things you have chosen to do?

Do you believe that you will reap what you sow? Even more,
have you experienced the principle of reaping and sowing?

What consequences are you reaping, and
how are you experiencing forgiveness?

How does it feel knowing God wants to use your story and allow
the choices you have made (good and bad) to bring hope to others?

I never want to live under condemnation for the life of sin I have lived.
But I also never want to forget the love and grace God gave me the day
He rescued me. How about you? What do you want to remember about
your rescue from the sin that can bring destruction?

Mile
Markers

—

When you think about one of your greatest regrets, what would you say was the foundation of your choice? In other words, what was the real reason you chose to go down a path that ended with shame, guilt or regret?

Identify a time when you made one of the best decisions you have ever made. What was the motivation behind choosing that path? How did that path lead you to experience life with love, peace and joy?

How can you be certain the choices you are making in your current race will produce the fruit of hope, love, self- control, and a stronger faith in God?

Mental Preparation

—

Remember, the Apostle Paul was known for murdering anyone who followed Jesus before he became a follower himself. In his letter to the church in Philippi he says:

"...Forgetting what lies behind and straining forward to what lies ahead..."

Philippians 3:13 (ESV)

What you think will determine what you will do, and
what you do will determine the direction you choose.
How have you seen this to be true in your own life?

How important are the thoughts you think about God?
How do your thoughts about God impact your choosing
to ask His direction over your life?

Do you think Paul was speaking from experience? How did
remembering his past benefit Paul's faith and ministry?

If we are going to run the race God has set for us and live the life Jesus has died to give us, we must be careful with the thoughts we allow into our mind. If you have ever struggled with negative thinking, you understand how important it is to be careful about every thought you allow to stay in your mind.

I'm not talking about making sure we have "positive" thoughts. A child of God must discern what are biblical truths and guard our minds with thoughts that are based on this truth. Biblical truths lead us to glorify God, not build up our fleshly desires.

How important is it for you to renew your mind? How does renewing your mind help you live the life God has for you now, not the life you used to live?

Read Romans 8:5-6 and jot down the different mindsets described in these verses. It's amazing how the mind expresses what is truly in the heart!

Heart Monitor

—

The finish of my half-marathon was not a pretty picture. I was so dehydrated and weak that I collapsed and lost consciousness. I was rushed to the emergency room, and my family was left with worry and panic. This was the price I paid for the choices I made. I was literally fighting for my life. In my Christian race, the lack of training I had in knowing God's Word, understanding the heart of God, and what it meant to be a follower of Jesus had left me tired, weary, and wanting to walk away from the God who loved me. I chose to drink from woman-made wells rather than from the living water Jesus offered. In both of these races, the lack of nourishing water affected how I finished. The problem came from a heart issue.

**Do you know what it means to come to the end
of yourself? Describe it in the space provided.**

If you have gotten to that place, how did faith in God revive you?

Nutrition & Hydration

—

The only way to satisfy the longing of our hearts is to sip on the truth written and saved for us in Scripture. When we slow down to sip on the truth of God's Word, our minds and souls begin to fill with life-giving, life-changing truths.

Take the truths below and renew your mind and heart by reading the verses out loud or writing them on an index card. I try to memorize God's Word as if He is speaking to me personally. I often pray what I believe God is saying in the verses I have chosen and then ask myself, "Do I believe this?"

Philippians 4:4-9

Romans 6:1-10

When I came across the finish line, I almost died. I was given another chance to live again. When I came to the end of myself in my Christian life, I had to die to myself. If I'm to live, it has to be for Christ. Drink from the verses in Romans 6 and notice how many times we are told to die to self and to live for Christ. Now read Romans 8 about a new life that is lived through the Spirit. Think about this, sip on this, and allow these truths to penetrate every part of your heart.

Community

Think about this:

Do not be deceived: God is not mocked, for whatever one sows, that will he also reap.

Galatians 6:7 (ESV)

Remember our principle for this chapter:

Every choice we make will impact not only our lives but also the lives of the people we love.

Sometimes we make decisions that negatively affect us and those around us. This means we have the capacity to cause harm to someone or be on the receiving end of someone else's bad choices. But God has never allowed anyone to hurt one of His children without paying the consequences. Remember, forgiveness does not remove consequences. We reap what we sow.

Read Acts 7:54-58 concerning the stoning of Stephen. Scripture clearly says when Jesus died, he sat down at the right hand of the Father. When Stephen was being stoned, Stephen saw Jesus standing. Jesus pays attention when someone throws a stone to hurt His children. Even if the stone is an accusation or a lie that pierces the heart, Jesus knows!

**Who is running beside you, encouraging you to
run the race God has mapped out for you?**

**Who (or what) might be attempting to
pull your eyes away from Jesus?**

Rest & Recovery

—

I have discovered that confessing, repenting, and receiving His forgiveness will provide the rest and recovery I need for my soul.

I want to encourage you to go back and reflect on the truths presented in this chapter. It is our faith in Jesus that allows us to rest in Him. The only way our bodies can recover and live the life God offers is to apply His truth and then abide in Him through obedience. Remember, obedience brings rest. Just as the woman at the well poured herself out in the presence of Jesus, we can pour out all we have and know that He can fill us with living water and restore our strength with His presence.

After reading this chapter and going deeper into His truth that
he choices we make will impact everyone around us, do you feel
God is asking you to confess, repent, and receive His forgiveness?

CHAPTER EIGHT

Do You Know Your Name?

IF WE ARE TO RUN AND FOLLOW
JESUS CONSISTENTLY, WE MUST
KNOW THE TRUTH OF WHO HE IS AND
WHO HE SAYS WE ARE IN HIM.

No, in all these things we are
more than conquerors through
him who loved us.

Romans 8:37 (ESV)

If someone asked me to choose a phrase that best described my race as a child of God, I would never have said that I was "more than a conqueror." Why is it that there's such a difference between how God describes His children and how His children see themselves? As I lay flat on my face after the race, no one was thinking, "She conquered that half-marathon!" The same is true of the many times I have failed to live faithfully as a child of God. I had a hard time believing I was more than a conqueror.

I'm embarrassed to admit how long I had been a follower of Jesus before I understood that God didn't call me a conqueror. It's the power of Jesus within me that allows me to be more than a conqueror; it's all IN HIM! Jesus is the conqueror, and I allow Him to conquer through me. Together, we walk in victory.

As followers of Jesus, we walk in victory when we first understand who we are in Christ, and then confess as sin what we've done that doesn't reflect this truth.

Do you know the truth of who you are as a child of God?

Your Race Your Life Your Story

—

Do you find it difficult to surrender your will to the Father's will? Read how difficult it was for Jesus in Luke 22:39-44. Can you remember the last time you prayed until the sweat off your face turned to blood? I have never prayed with that amount of intensity! Have you?

On another note, when was the last time you fell flat on your fac from trying to be the perfect person, the perfect Christian, or the perfect _____(fill in the blank)?

The paramedics asked me if I knew my name and if I knew what I had done. The answers I gave him determined my degree of health at that point. If I didn't know my name or what I had just finished, I was in deep physical trouble.

After trying so hard to live the Christian life and failing miserably, I needed to answer the same two questions.

> *"Do you know who you are in Christ?"*
> *"Do you realize what you have done?"*

No child of God is exempt from answering these questions. Knowing who we are in Christ is essential to approaching God as His child and walking in obedience with Him. Knowing what we have done is essential to walking in freedom and victory. Freedom and victory are ours as we confess our sins and receive the gift of forgiveness from Jesus.

Think about this:

As children of God, if we don't know who God says we are and don't agree with and embrace this truth, we will never feel good enough to approach a holy God.

If we don't confess what we have done and agree with God that we have sinned against Him, we will never understand grace, mercy, hope, and unconditional love.

The exchange of our old life for our new spiritual life brings a new identity by being in Christ. Did you know when you were "born again" God gave you a new identity as His child?

Read 2 Corinthians 5:17-21 and ask yourself, "Does this represent who I am and how I live my life?"

Would you consider your life one that reflects the power of God, or one that reflects your own weakness?

Mile Markers

—

In the book, I share how difficult it is for me to accept being weak. I wanted to be strong. I thought God wanted me to be strong. But the truth is, God wants me to become weak so that, in my weakness, He is strong. If I seek strength from myself, I'm at odds with God who has allowed my weakness so He can make me strong. You can see this in 2 Corinthians 12:9 (check this out!)

When I think about mile markers, I think about the many times I came to a very important turning point in my life. The choices I made often determined the life I lived. What about you? What major events have happened in your life that may have made it difficult for you to accept God's forgiveness?

Is it easier for you to accept God's forgiveness than it is to forgive yourself?

Thinking back over some of your mile markers, how often have you wanted to forget the moments when you felt the most vulnerable and weak?

How does knowing God wants you to embrace your weakness and call upon Him change the way you see those moments?

When I was "picked up" by the paramedics and placed in the ambulance, I had to face the reality that things were not turning out as I had planned.

In what ways has life turned out the way you thought it would?

In what ways does life look much different than you thought it would?

Are you at a place in your life where you feel confident
you're running the race God has set for you? Share
some of the ways God is confirming this for you.

If not, what are some things you can do to get back in the race God has set for you?

Mental Preparation

—

A divine exchange took place when we made a new covenant with our heavenly Father through confession of our faith in Jesus. He gave us His character and His nature. All that He is became ours. But we will never walk in this truth and experience all the treasures given to us in Jesus if we do not change our thinking.

Ask God to replace the old thinking with the truth given to you as a new creation in Christ.
I have found that we run toward what we keep our minds on. Our thoughts will be the force that will direct our path.

Read and think on Proverbs 21:29.

In the half-marathon, I had the wrong understanding of what it meant to be a runner in a very difficult race. My wrong thinking brought me the wrong results. This was also true as a follower of Jesus. I had the wrong understanding of what it meant to follow Jesus and be born again.

How about meditating on this:

And we know that the Son of God has come and has given us understanding, so that we may know him who is true, and we are in him who is true, in his Son Jesus Christ. He is the true God and eternal life.

1 John 5:20 (ESV)

List a few of the lies you have believed about
who you are as a new creation in Christ.

List a few of the lies you have believed about
the heart of God and His will for your life.

How can you change the way you view
what it means to be "new creation?"

Heart Monitor

Crossing the finish line, I could not stand or keep myself from falling. Because of the poor choices I made, my desire to go on was no longer strong enough to keep me from falling flat on my face.

Did you know God looks at our hearts while man looks at our behavior? It's easy to be trained in what to do, but God is more concerned with what motivates our behavior: the heart.

Have you experienced how difficult it is to keep moving forward when your heart is breaking?

Write a one sentence description of each truth found in these verses:

Deuteronomy 11:16

Psalm 19:14

Psalm 27:3, 8, 14

Matthew 15:18

Luke 6:45

Nutrition & Hydration

—

Here are a few truths about who Jesus is and who we are as Christ followers:

God is Abba, Father.
Romans 8:15-16

I am Abba's child.
Romans 8:15-16

God is my hiding place.
Psalm 32:7

My life is hidden with Christ.
Colossians 3:3

Jesus is the beloved Son of God.
Matthew 3:17

I am accepted in the beloved.
Ephesians 1:6

Jesus is the Lamb who shed the blood that cleanses me from sin.
1 John 1:7b

I am clean in Jesus.
John 15:3

Jesus is our advocate.
1 John 2:1

I know that God is for me.
Romans 8:31

Jesus is my hope.
1 Timothy 1:1

My hope is fixed.
Romans 15:4, 13

God is good.
Psalm 100:5

I know all things work for good.
Romans 8:28

Don't just read these truths, but allow them to soak into your heart, letting the living water quench your thirsty heart.

Community

When I fell at the finish line, I felt alone. The lady watching me was helpless, even though she knew I was falling and in danger. The people around us have limited ability to help keep us from falling. Yes, a friend who is not afraid to speak truth into our lives is valuable, but it's up to us to live out the truth.

I have seen more Christians fall surrounded by other Christians than by non-believers. I have often wondered why that seems to be true, and I can't help but think we let our guards down when we are surrounded by only Christians. If we are with non-believers, often we want to be a Godly example. I don't think this is 100% true all the time, but it's more true than I ever thought possible. Has this been your experience as well?

I agree with what Kenneth Boa wrote about commitment to community when he said,

"As believers grow in the solitude of intimacy with the Lord, their capacity for life in community increases as well. True community in Christ is not a collection of lonely or isolated individuals but a dynamic interaction of people who know they are accepted and beloved in Christ." [1]

Remember, friends, family or other Christians can only encourage and speak truth to us. It's up to us to choose to know Him truthfully, to follow Him faithfully, and to love Him unconditionally.

Be careful not to allow anyone but God define who you are! It's important that we surround ourselves with people who understand they are accepted and beloved children of God.

[1]Boa, Kenneth. Conformed to His Image. (Zondervan, 2001)

Do you have a community of people surrounding
you who understand who they are in Christ?

Who are you finding community with?

Rest & Recovery

—

Read through the truths listed and
find rest and healing for your soul:

I am a child of God.
John 1:12

I have been justified and redeemed.
Romans 3:24

My old self was crucified with Christ.
Romans 6:6

I have been set free from the law of sin and death.
Romans 8:2

I have been accepted by Christ.
Romans 15:7

I have been brought near to God by the blood of Christ.
Ephesians 2:13

I have become the righteousness of God in Christ.
2 Corinthians 5:21

I am a new creation in Christ.
2 Corinthians 5:17

Do you know your name? Do you know what you have done?

Sit and sip on the truth of who you are in Christ.

CHAPTER NINE

Free to Run

THE KEY TO WALKING & RUNNING IN
FREEDOM IS OBEDIENCE.

He gives power to the faint, and to him who has no might he increases strength. Even youths shall faint and be weary, and young men shall fall exhausted; but they who wait for the LORD shall renew their strength; they shall mount up with wings like eagles; they shall run and not be weary; they shall walk and not faint.

Isaiah 40:29-31 (ESV)

Every time I share my half-marathon story, it reminds me of the power of choice. God created us, and in His sovereignty, He gave us the power to choose. I had no idea my choices of not training, going at a pace I was not trained to run, and not drinking water would leave me helpless and fighting for my life. I finished that race and immediately started the race for survival. The day I went to the hospital I was told two people died after running the same half-marathon I had just finished. I was close to becoming the third victim.

Have you heard anyone say, "What you don't know won't hurt you?"That's a lie! As a matter of fact, what you don't know may not only hurt you, it may kill you!

In the moments after the race, my life was measured by the condition of my heart. Training to know how to run a half-marathon or drinking water to hydrate my body was no longer the issue. I was in danger of having a heart problem.

The same is true when we decide to follow Jesus. We have a heart problem! God wants us to know, love, and follow Jesus with an undivided heart. I tried to live the Christian life by my own rules.

When my rules didn't give me the life I desired, I tried to seek God. I loved Him, but I happened to also love life on my own terms more. I had no concept of the power of the Holy Spirit or how to walk in freedom and victory as a child of God, but I had to get to that place before I was willing to give God my whole heart.

He lovingly picked me up, offered me another chance to run with Him, for Him, and because of Him. I was thirsty for more of Him, and every day I have learned the importance of looking to Jesus and receiving the living water He provides.

How do we get this living water Jesus offers? Simply pray and seek Him with all your heart. Prayer is essential, and the truths written in Scripture—truths about how to train to be faithful followers of Jesus with pure hearts—have been given to all of us.

What about you? Do you have a story of falling on your face while trying to be a "good" Christian? Are you thirsty for more than this life can offer? Do you want to know what it means to love God with all your heart?

Your Race
Your Life
Your Story

—

Who or what do you love with all your heart?

It's hard to love God with all your heart when everything around you is competing for your devotion. Do you agree? What are some things that compete for your whole heart?

How have you tried to live the Christian life in your own strength?

Mile Markers

—

I'm not one to focus on the past. I think we can learn from it, but if we look behind us too long, we will repeat the past. That being said, we can learn from the different obstacles satan throws at us so we can recognize the ways he tries to rob us from enjoying the love of Jesus.

Have you considered retracing the steps in
your life that have led you away from God?

What are some big events or circumstances in your life that you thought
were good at the time but eventually became some of your greatest regrets?

How can you see the hand of God leading and encouraging you to keep
running? Do you see how He allows the good and bad moments to become
life-giving "mile markers" as evidence of His power in your life?

Mental Preparation

—

I believe one of the greatest struggles we will encounter is in our minds. Freedom and victory are often determined in our minds before we ever take a step forward. Negative thinking can keep us from trusting God to use all our circumstances as powerful tools to help others.

Maybe this negative thinking is based on past experiences or harmful words spoken over you. No matter the source, we must renew our minds with the words of God's truth, not the lies others have spoken.

In my half-marathon, I embraced the lie that I didn't need to train or drink water in order to be qualified to run. In my spiritual race, I believed the lie that I wasn't good enough or loved by the people I wanted to love me. Nor did I expect God to give me the desires of my heart.

In what ways do you struggle with negative thinking?

How have your negative thoughts kept you from moving
forward and taking hold of all God has for you?

The mind is a powerful part of your body that God has created.
He knows that what goes in our minds will often determine our
choices. How has your mind affected the direction of your life?

What would you say is the most life-threatening lie you
have believed about yourself and God?

Through this study, has God revealed any lie you have embraced about
who you are as His child and/ or the truth concerning His heart for you?

Heart Monitor

Research has proven that our thoughts often dictate our feelings. Have you ever been in a good mood and, within minutes of a negative comment, or comparing yourself to someone you admire, you begin feeling inadequate and defeated?

It is important to check the condition of our hearts and take every precaution to keep them free from bitterness and deceitfulness. We never know when we will face a difficult path or an unexpected mountain to climb.

In the Nutrition and Hydration section, there are several truths that connect the importance of protecting our minds and hearts. Remember, man looks on the outside of a person, but God looks in our hearts.

Have you ever been in a good mood and, within minutes of a negative comment, or comparing yourself to someone you admire, you begin feeling inadequate and defeated?

What thoughts, circumstances, or words spoken over you have made it hard to trust God to change your life?

Have you taken any specific measures to protect your heart from discouragement, fear, or anything that has the potential of robbing you from loving God with all your heart? If so, what are they?

Nutrition & Hydration

—

God has given us truth upon truth about the importance of protecting our hearts from anything that can lead us away from His heart. Here are a few verses to look up and meditate on. I highly suggest you "take to heart" all God is saying so that you will not lose heart in doing good.

Proverbs 3:5

Proverbs 4:23

Matthew 5:8

Mark 7:20-21

Romans 8:26-27

2 Corinthians 4:16-18

Philippians 4:7

Colossians 2:2

Community

Have you ever tried to live someone else's life? One that looks different than the life you've been given? How has that worked for you?

Since God has given you the grace and power to live the life He created especially for you, how do you feel when you compare yourself to someone else or try to live their life instead?

Who is the godliest influence in your life at the moment?

What intentional steps have they given you to protect your heart from embracing the lies the world is throwing at you on a daily basis?

Rest & Recovery

—

Take a verse from the list in the Nutrition & Hydration section and ask God to reveal His truth in a deeper way. Then rest in this truth by applying it to your life. Obedience to God's word brings freedom. To live and enjoy freedom is to rest and recover in the grace and mercy of God.

After my half-marathon, I was placed on a stretcher and put in an ambulance where they pumped me with IV fluids. I finished the race, but I didn't finish strong. It was only when I became weak that I was in a position to find all I needed to become strong. The same is true as a follower of Jesus. I had to empty myself of myself before I had space in my life for God to fill me with His Spirit. In my weakness, He is made strong. I had to admit I was not strong before I was willing to embrace His strength and find rest in Him.

How about you? Are you struggling to be strong when God wants you to become weak? God can replace your limited abilities with His never ending strength when you are willing to humble yourself and ask Him.

To find freedom, rest, and recovery in Him is to be willing to admit you are weak. Allow His Spirit to fill the emptiness of your heart and soul with His power.

Are you resting in Him?

CHAPTER TEN

Your Final Race

THE KEY TO FINISHING STRONG IS TO
EXCHANGE LIVING IN THE MOMENT FOR
LIVING WITH AN ETERNAL PERSPECTIVE.

I have fought the good fight,
I have finished the race,
I have kept the faith.

2 Timothy 4:7 (ESV)

What's the difference between The Finish Line and The Final Race? The fact is that we are all running in some type of race every day, and until God calls us home, we must keep running!

Have you said, "If I can only get through this _____?"

As long as we are on this earth, we will finish one season (race) and maybe get a break for a few days or months. Then life happens, and we are right back to running. We cross over one finish line to enjoy a few days rest until God allows our circumstances to change and sets us off to run another race.

Steve Farrar writes in his book, *Finishing Strong*, that it's not how you start life that matters, but how you finish:

"Several years ago Howard Hendricks (Dallas Seminary Professor) conducted a study of 246 men in full-time ministry who experienced personal moral failure within a two year period. In other words, Hendricks was able to find nearly 250 men who derailed within twenty-four months of being in full-time ministry. That's roughly ten a month for two years. Ten guys a month in moral failure. That's almost three guys a week, and each of them started strong!"[2]

This must break the heart of God. Do you agree?

[2]Farrar, Steve. Finishing Strong. (Multnomah, 2000)

Your Race
Your Life
Your Story

—

Have you experienced a time in your life when you wanted to walk away from God?

Did you walk away, or did you resist the temptation and keep running?

Name a few of the races (circumstances in your life) you have had to run in the past few years and rate them in intensity using the following categories: easy, mild, hard, or impossible.

Race: Race:

Intensity: Intensity:

Race: Race:

Intensity: Intensity:

Race: Race:

Intensity: Intensity:

Read chapter 13 from the book of Numbers.

How many spies went out?How many remained faithful and listened to God?

The spies in Numbers 13 sound a lot like the survey Howard Hendricks presented. Why do you think Christians get so discouraged in their Christian life? What could possibly tempt them to walk away from the faith?

How can we become a "Joshua and Caleb" instead of
following the pattern 3 of the other 10 spies?

Remember this: Each spy was a leader. These spies were the
best of the best! It just goes to show us that no one is above
failure, and God can use even the not-so-pretty moments to
encourage us and remind us to always look to Him.

How can God use your story to encourage others
to keep the faith when life seems so hard?

Mile
Markers

—

Do you think you can fully understand what it means to trust God if you never experience setbacks, trials, or difficult circumstances in your life?

Have you been encouraged by others as you've watched them trust God during very painful and difficult circumstances?

I have discovered that my response to trials is often dependent on my understanding of the goodness of God. How have you seen this to be true in your own experience?

How would you describe your initial response to God when you face trials?

Spend some time reading and meditating on each of these things and ask God to give you a greater understanding of what He is saying:

Endurance (James 1:3)

Steadfastness (1 Corinthians 15:58)

Thanksgiving (1 Thessalonians 5:18)

Diligence, moral excellence, self-control, perseverance, and godliness (2 Peter 1:5-6)

Compassion (Colossians 3:12)

Faithfulness (Galatians 5:22)

Whenever you face a huge mile marker in your life and you are too tired to keep going, Isaiah the prophet has a few encouraging words to help you to keep running:

Have you not known? Have you not heard? The LORD is the everlasting God, the Creator of the ends of the earth. He does not faint or grow weary, his understanding is unsearchable. He gives power to the faint, and to him who has no might he increases strength. Even youths shall faint and be weary, and young men shall fall exhausted; but they who wait for the LORD shall renew their strength, they shall mount up with wings like eagles; they shall run and not be weary, they shall walk and not faint.

Isaiah 40:28-31 (ESV)

Mental Preparation

In the book, I shared with you the choice to not train or drink water and to run at a pace that assured I would stay in the race instead of getting swept up before finishing. Every choice in my mind seemed right at the moment. My thoughts affected my behavior, and my behavior determined the outcome of my race.

Read the words that King Solomon shares with you:

Proverbs 14:12
Proverbs 16:25
Proverbs 18:17

Do you think a person's perspective on suffering has anything to do with their ability to finish strong? In what ways?

How might your perspective on the goodness of God play a vital part in your own ability to finish strong?

Do you get the idea Solomon is speaking from his own experience? What are the warnings he is trying to tell us?

When it is hard for me to have a godly perspective, I read and meditate on one or all of these verses. If you are having a hard time renewing your mind and having godly thoughts, try focusing your thoughts on these verses:

Philippians 4:8

Ephesians 3:20

Galatians 6:3

2 Corinthians 10:5

1 Corinthians 10:12

Romans 12:3

James 1:26

Heart Monitor

—

I have found the greatest barrier to loving God is a lack of knowing Him. I have asked God on a daily basis to help me to know Him, to love Him, and to allow me to follow Him. If we truly knew Him, we would unconditionally love Him. And if we unconditionally love Him, we will faithfully follow Him. Do you agree?

I think Paul would agree!
Read the following chapters:

Ephesians 1 and 3
Philippians 1
Colossians 1

What would you consider your greatest barrier to enjoying a
close relationship with Jesus and loving God with all your heart?

What is the overall theme of each of these chapters?

Nutrition & Hydration

One of my favorite books is *Conformed To His Image* by Kenneth Boa. In the conclusion of his book, he asks the questions, "What does it take to finish well? How do we keep the faith?" Looking at Hebrews 12:1, he lists a few of his observations of people who run with endurance the race that is set before them. I think it's worth our time to think about these seven observations in people who have kept the faith and finished well:

Intimacy with Christ.
(Love Jesus with all your heart.)

Fidelity in the spiritual disciplines.
(Bible study and prayer are two.)

A biblical perspective on the circumstances of life.
(See through God's eyes.)

A teachable, responsive, humble, and obedient spirit.
(Open your heart to hear from God.)

A clear sense of personal purpose and calling.
(Living the life God has called you to live.)

Healthy relationships with resourceful people.
(Be careful who you listen to and spend time with.)

Ongoing ministry investment in the lives of others. (Living life with an eternal perspective.)[3]

The seven key words are:

1. Intimacy

2. Disciplines

3. Perspective

4. Teachable

5. Purpose

6. Relationship

7. Ministry

Think on these seven observations and ask God to show you which you need to apply to your life. Here are a few great verses to help you renew your mind and refresh your soul:

Hebrews 12:10-11

1 Peter 4:12-17

2 Corinthians 1:3-5

2 Corinthians 4:16-18

Acts 20:24-33

1 Corinthians 9:24-27

[3]Boa, Kenneth. *Conformed to His Image.* (Zondervan, 2001)

Community

Research shows that few people who start to follow Jesus in their twenties will stay on track and continue following Him into old age.

Have you heard of or do you know anyone personally who started strong in their Christian race only to quit and walk away from the faith?

What about people who had what appeared to be a wonderful life, but who made some bad choices that brought regret and the end of their storybook life?

Are there people who had zero chance of a good life by our worldly standards, but against all odds, their life was redeemed and they decided to follow Jesus and finish strong?

How can you fuel your desire to keep the faith and run your race faithfully?

Who can you ask to hold you accountable as you run?

Rest & Recovery

—

Rest and recover in these truths as you read Hebrews 9:27-28.

I love Max Lucado's metaphor of entering into heaven. Every time I read it in his book *The Applause of Heaven* I'm reminded of the joy I will experience when I see my mom and dad again in heaven. But nothing can compare to seeing the face of Jesus, whom I have given my heart and soul to. I can't imagine what it will be like to hear the applause of the angels or to see Jesus rise from His throne to welcome me home! If we can keep the perspective that this life is not our home, we will continue to live the life God has called us to live without becoming tired, weary, and eventually quitting.

When I was in the ambulance and finally able to speak, I asked the paramedics if I had received my medal. I have thought about this so often. If I was so concerned with getting my cheap Disney medal, how much more will I want to receive my eternal rewards?

One day (and I have no idea when) I will look in the face of Jesus, who saved my life far more completely than the wonderful paramedics, and He will hand me my eternal rewards. This thought alone should motivate us to keep running with Jesus and for Jesus.

Jesus is our life. Each day we have the choice to embrace Him-to embrace life-and run the race marked out for us.

Here is where we can finally find rest:

John 14:2-3 (ESV)
In my Father's house are many rooms. If it were not so, would
I have told you that I go to prepare a place for you?
And if I go and prepare a place for you, I will come again and
will take you to myself, that where I am you may be also.

1 Corinthians 2:9 (ESV)
But, as it is written, "What no eye has seen, nor ear heard, nor
the heart of man imagined, what God has prepared for those
who love him."

2 Corinthians 4:17 (ESV)
For this light momentary affliction is preparing for us an
eternal weight of glory
beyond all comparison.

*Until then... **KEEP RUNNING!***